The une

Alejandra Silva Romero

BookLeaf
Publishing

India | USA | UK

The unexpected © 2024 Alejandra Silva Romero

All rights reserved.

Alejandra Silva Romero asserts the moral right to be identified as the author of this work.

Presentation by *BookLeaf Publishing*

Web: www.bookleafpub.com

E-mail: info@bookleafpub.com

ISBN:9789358313697

First edition 2024

DEDICATION

To Patricia, my mother, who had to bear with reading hundreds of my poetries during the years. Thank you for your support and your objective opinion.

PREFACE

In this book, you will encounter some references
to The Dictionary of Obscure Sorrows by John
Koenig. As well as, two references of very
famous paintings made by Leonardo da Vinci
(Mona Lisa) and Michelangelo Merisi da
Caravaggio (The boy bitten by a lizard).

Loneliness

Under the rain
Without shelter
Nowhere to stay
Things could be better

The strength of the wind misleads me
Lightning flashes that make me jumpy
Half-closed eyes, I see headlights blurry
Rumbling and whispers that I try to flee
Narrow street reflected by a glow in the dark
This piercing light that brushes against my back
The one I avoid hiding behind my coat
Spotlights and glances that I loathe

Puddle to puddle
I run in a park
Sudden eerie makes its mark
Then, I stop, I'm muddled
Then, I look at the moon that watches quietly
Ragged breathing
Thirst intensifying
My eyes drift down slowly
My soul catches pieces of the pale light
Truth, shed sympathy
Lies exhausted by the fight

Reflection of my soul
In a puddle, instantly overwhelmed.
Empty look, sad and abandoned
A look where cries rule.

Mona Lisa

The canvas was small in a giant room
Between visitors, I saw your true colours
The most famous painting, yet so common
No distortion of the true core

Youthfulness who irradiates a golden
complexion
Through your small mysterious narrowed eyes
Soft finesse of your face elongated by your
nose's lines
Your curly dark brown hair fight to strand
dominion

Curious woman, seated in the middle of moors
Surrounded by a landscape with multiple
meanders
Surreal nature in the light of thunders,
Elegantly rested as a saint with such pallor

Dressed in refined fabrics unveiling vivid
pigments
Complementary shades that are diligent
A detail in your face reflects cheerfulness
One timeless prowess
A slight smirk

And people make up any kind of quirks.

Boy bitten by a lizard

You were the smallest painting in the room,
hanging on the wall
The colours were dull, and the subject was
blurry
I had to take a guess of the painter's goal
That face? Which gender? Androgyny.

That expression. Surprised? In pain?
Ugliest portrait, no grace, no beauty
Prettiest portrait, full of mysteries and
singularity
Flowers of innocence refusing to be tamed

Crystalline jar flowing desires to quench my
thirst
No artificial lights, just the sun lord marking his
territory
A lizard mingled with the background, quickly
Gets her back to reality, pinching to end indecent
lusts

Magical masterpiece playing with movement
It's simply symbolic
Ridiculous, was my comment
Finding in it, inspiration, and lyrics.

Little brats

Crashy teens in this crappy school
Monday already, salty mood
Boys flexing like dummies
Girls looking yassified
Let them laugh, let them smoke
Low-key lazy bums with no future
Gloomy faces and throwing shade
I can't wait for the next cocky teen I'll break

Weird, idiot, out of place
Everything to toughen them up
Unworthy of encouragement
Everything to make them grow up
Crushing dreams and putting hardships
It's been like this forever, we are not changing
the codes

I need to pay my bills
I'll keep facing these dreadful brats, even if that
kills

Dear teacher,
I hope this poetry finds you well.
See, students are blossoming in different ways

Why would you crush a bud that'll become a
unique flower
Would you be so kind as to restraint your
bitterness
See, your opinion is not requested
Although empathy would be much appreciated.

Kind regards,
> Discard

Black leather jacket

Change of life, change of style
Thrift shop on the corner
Brushing pass the clothes of the aisle
Trending fits in the same order
Something caught my eye
Vintage black leather jacket
Perfect choice to blend in
Perfect image on to lean
Teenage issues are starting to set
Everybody's jacket is the best accessory
It feels amazing
Everybody talks to you
Everybody looks at you
It's new on you
People approve, that's what you wanted
Tonight, it will be another story.
Looking at your reflection, it is but only you
Old self outcast but true
You feel the confidence wear off
You can't hide when things get tough
Sudden urge of burning the jacket
Stomping on it
Tear it down piece by piece
Is the ticket to society worth the peace?

Whispers

You left at the perfect moment
No one was paying attention
As always, it's a bad end
Heart beating sensation
One step more
Still breathing
Who cares if you are a whore
When men are watching
You become a thing
Keep inside your childhood
Act like if you were something
The truth, they don't want to know
Crying is for weak people
Too bad for you
If your parents aren't able
To ask: "How are you ?"

Letters

She used to write you
Poems of melancholy
Wrote hidden rhymes to find clues
I remember her staying up until three
In the morning, for you

Far, far away, but needing to be close
Seeking to be seen meddled with prose
Her heart would ache, but she knew
You'll understand what she goes through

She would bear the pain
If it meant him giving her a glance
She would settle for crazy while being sane
Shatter her dreams slowly building up a fence

Never good at talking
The only thing she could do is keep writing
Submerged by agony
She would question why this is her destiny

One day, I saw the recipient opening his letter
box
Between ads and taxes, a handwritten hope
Looking closely, he recognized the paradox

Rolled his eyes and threw away the envelope.

Synaesthesia

Bittersweet orange notes mixed with magnolia
and rose fragrance
Inhaling this symphony of complementary
colours
I perceive smoky waves crossing my mind
Shaping figures embalmed by indistinct lines

It feels a bit cosmical, colour into the darkness
White stars shattering to pieces of crystal
I pick the solid material that feels like a flower
fragile
But the sharp acid taste of orange cuts the
process

—"It makes me think of the oranges my
grandmother peeled for me in the countryside."
People around me display their memories with
pride
I can't quiet my senses, everything is a new
experience
But people around won't understand the
difference

I contemplate the sound that rings in my ears
Suave melody followed by a legato rhythm

Rose and magnolia overflowed by the cloud's
tears
Staccato keys of first spring drops prism

Some would say it's like wizardry
Struck by omniscient perception
Clearly driven by sickening motions.

Coherent writing

My
Syntax
Is
Right

Right
Is
My
Syntax

Syntax
Is
Right
My

Right
My
Syntax
Is

My syntax is right
Little matter consonants,
Punctuations, figures of speech
Structure serving the meaning isn't cheap.

The draft of writers

Apparently, my handwriting is tiny
Same dimensions of fly's legs
Narrow their eyes to read me
Unworthy of their effort's head.

Apparently, my writing is choppy
Lines too long for their content
Words are spaced ridiculously
Reading it, doesn't merit an intent

Apparently, my writing is sloppy
Scribbles more similar to hieroglyphs
It burns their eyes to glance at this atrophy
Rumour runs that me knowing cursive is a myth

A way of writing that describes personality
Hundreds of authors' drafts would agree
Critics seem uptight
To a similar pen of masterpieces that saw the
light.

Placebo

Hello doctor, I'm sick
Strangely, I feel good
Life seems less dull
But they say I need to be fixed

Doctor, is it serious?
What's your hopeless diagnostic?
I can finally feel, that's curious
I wouldn't dare to ask for prognostics

Doctor, I think I feel alive
No headaches, no stomach pain anymore
You keep saying I need meds to thrive
But doctor, I feel better than before

Doctor says no.
He's the one that's right
No listening to his patients
He's the cultivated man

I don't believe in your lure
Doctor, I am Diogenes
I'm waiting to be led
To an uncertain future.

Hyacinth

Simple bud of nature
Not a fan of flowers
But of you, I remember
Looking at you for hours

Strong and vigorous, you grew
Leaves coated of beautiful petals
Rare violet hybridisation new
Showing off its bloom that soon falls

Harsh autumn approaching
Your maturation ceases
Now, I can see you drying
Bits blown away by a simple breeze

Winter freezing snow
Knocks at people's doors
Moods are jolly or low
Surprising gift of yours

I see flakes on fresh foliage
Surreal flowers fighting the cold
Warmed up by the bulb sage
Thriving in a weather outside of the mould

Violet memory of an eight-year-old.

A sofa, a desk, and a chair

Hi Shrink! I'm Miss heartbroken
I bet you see a thousand of me
But you're the only one I'll tell my pain
I will pay you if you fix me,
If there's even a way
It started with a sad feeling
I ignored it; it should be okay
But one blind eye jeopardised my healing
A classic! I'm not sure how this will help
I can't stop talking while my heart sinks
I say words that my soul makes a mockery
I'm utterly numb, barely feeling a blink
My body is moving but I'm gone.
It feels heavy to carry myself on the streets
Tell me what's the true meaning of all this?
Go on.
Breaking this hellish cycle seems like a myth
"What am I here for?" You. Tell. Me.

Maugry/Paranoia

Dazed inside the crowd
My mind start running wild
I wonder if they know
Or avoid being raw

Talking with each other
Never with me
My words look scary
When I see their expression fluster

I wonder sometimes if it's just me
Or are they showing hypocrisy
Protecting my feelings
To not compromise my healing

Am I crazy?
Do I interpret signs that aren't there?
None of this torment is fair
In my mind, the truth is hazy.

Ne'er-be-gone/Nowhere home

Meeting strangers in every destination
Travelling around as a mission
Strong urge to discover
New things, that define me as explorer

Where am I going ?
Where am I from?
I don't remember.
I've tamed the change

Thirsty for more than one choice
Settling for nothing that bores
I keep running faster than the clouds
Telling stories out loud

Restless, it's my curse and my gift
I keep moving to avoid emptiness to burn
A gut feeling that would make me shift.
Habitant of the earth but no home to yearn.

Endzoned/After

People talk about desire as if it was an endless wait. Persevering in a path for so long that you even forget the goal. Philosophers ask us if desire is what gives our lives meaning. The wait makes the impatience grow; the exhilarating yearn of a promise. What happens when all your wishes are completed? Hoping for fulfilment and a sense of accomplishment. Nothing else to crave that will torture your nights. You got what you wanted. But now what? What happens after the people live happily ever after. What happens when the hero completes its quest? What happens in the end? All great adventures start from desire. Thinking we could finally reach a treasure of happiness. Instead, just plain content inspired my mind. No sense of greatness, nor forever joy to feel. Just a momentary satisfaction. Leaving a confused look on my face.

Typifice/Adaptation

She is an artichoke
She has layers
Change is for a few players
Willing to dig deep behind the cloak

My sister was resentful
Unforgiving of past mistakes
No second chances for any soul
She can't keep a façade, hates all that's fake

Lies after lies
Grew her disappointment
Silent cries
Breaking her judgement

Confronted by a choice
The one dilemma discuss before uproar
Peace or war
Internal conflict of remorse

Time passes but everything stays the same
She changed but the people haven't
They mention old wounds as your current shame
Fierce battle discredited in an instant.

Missing the boat

I didn't hesitate to get close to you. It wasn't a triviality talking with you. I didn't know how to act. I was shaking. Futile sentences. The fear persisted in my volatile heart. This romanticised cliché eventually decays. Tell me, are you interested? In progress… Then, nothing more to try when I saw our gaze decline. I don't understand these missed actions. Like confused intentions of subtle hypocrisy. I realised, late, that you only wanted to play a game that doesn't interest me. Enriched distressed illusions. I was there but I'm not anymore. It's you who lost. The second player declares forfeit.

Justing/If only

Had a child
Everything turned upside-down
Sudden atrocious fears
Overwhelming tears
Unborn child without any family
Baby dad doesn't love mummy
Not his first child
Reaction that was mild

Dad had another compromise. He is all that she
wants. Loving husband and father. Took them
away from adult problems. With not even a
glance, his face disappeared. After the
revelation, showed no compassion. If only he
would have loved her, perhaps the baby could
have a father.
Is that so?

The sleep train

I wait for my coach
Hearing in my head the noisy trailway
Mister train is bright red with tints of grey
I can hear the bell of his approach

You won't have to be late
When drowsiness hits, it'll call your name.
See his expression solid and dour
Because Mister train doesn't wait an hour

Missing your sleep train
Is frustrating.
The only thing I can hear now is pattering of
rain
Against the window, outside, pouring

Mister train will come back
Time to go when you hear the train tracks.

Back

With my thumb trailing up and down
Pressing the defined trait of the spine
I run my palm on his bulky shoulders
Shadows and lights emphasising the boulder

Asymmetrical harmony
Perfect thrill for any fantasy.